P9-BJC-549

Everyday History

Sending a Letter

ROWLAND HILL 1795-1879

Alex Stewart

W
FRANKLIN WATTS
A Division of Grolier Publishing
NEW YORK • LONDON • HONG KONG • SYDNEY
DANBURY, CONNECTICUT

Photographs:
4 Peter Newark's Western Americana, 5
Matthew McKee/Eye Ubiquitous, 6 E.T. archive, 8
Mary Evans Picture Library, 10 Peter Newark's Historical Pictures,
11 Mary Evans Picture Library, 12 Peter Newark's American
Pictures, 13 top and bottom Mary Evans Picture Library, 15 Peter
Newark's Western Americana, 16 Mary Evans Picture Library, 17
top Mary Evans Picture Library, 17 bottom Peter Newark's
Western Americana, 18 Peter Newark's Pictures, 20 top Peter
Newark's American Pictures, 20 bottom Mary Evans Picture
Library, 21 Peter Newark's Historical Pictures, 22 Mary Evans
Picture Library, 24 E.T. archive, 25 Mary Evans Picture Library, 28
Peter Hendrie/Image Bank.

Acknowledgement
Discovery Books would like to thank Federal Express for the loan
of material.

Planning and production by Discovery Books Limited
Editors: Paul Humphrey, Claire Berridge
Design: Ian Winton
Art Director: Robert Walster
Illustrators: Ross Watton, Stefan Chabluk, Terry Hadler, Joanna
Williams

Visit Franklin Watts/Children's Press on the Internet at:
http://publishing.grolier.com

First published in 1999
by Franklin Watts

First American edition 1999 by Franklin Watts/Children's Press
A Division of Grolier Publishing
90 Sherman Turnpike
Danbury, CT 06816

Library of Congress Cataloging-in-Publication Data
Stewart, Alex.
    Sending a Letter / Alex Stewart.
        p.   cm. -- (Everyday History)
    Includes index.
    Summary: Describes how messages have been sent
throughout history, from the use of smoke signals and messengers
to modern use of electronic means of communication, including
fax and email.
        ISBN 0-531-14547-6 (hbk)
            0-531-15401-7 (pbk)
    1. Postal service--History--Juvenile literature. 2. Mail
receiving and forwarding services--History--Juvenile literature. [1.
Postal service--History.] I. Title. II. Series.
HE6076.S74 2000
383'.14'09--dc21   99-17172
                                                              CIP

GROLIER
PUBLISHING

Contents

Sending Messages

Most of us enjoy getting letters in the mail. It is fun writing back to our family and friends, too. Many children have pen pals in other countries. Every day, all over the world, mail men and women deliver millions of letters.

A mail woman delivers letters in Sydney, Australia.

Before Writing

There was a time when people didn't write any letters at all. There weren't any pens, paper, stamps, or envelopes, either. In fact, there wasn't even any writing.

Before writing was invented, people still sent messages. They blew loud musical instruments, such as horns. Their sound was used to warn of danger.

Smoke Signals

Some Native American people used smoke signals to send simple messages. Other native peoples beat out messages on drums.

Messengers

Before writing was invented, the best way to send long messages was by messenger. A messenger had to be a fast runner with a good memory. His work could be dangerous. Messengers who brought bad news sometimes had their heads cut off!

The First Postal Services

Rulers in ancient times used messengers to carry letters around their kingdoms. The first letters were delivered one at a time. The ancient Egyptians started the first postal service 4,000 years ago. It used a network of messengers to carry official mail.

In ancient times few people knew how to write. Even kings and queens needed scribes to write letters for them. This Sumerian scribe is writing on clay tablets with a reed pen.

A Sumerian scribe.

Something to Write On

The ancient Egyptians invented the first kind of paper. It was made from water reeds and was called papyrus. Early writers also wrote on parchment, made from dried animal skins. Tsai Lun, a Chinese man, invented the first proper paper about 2,000 years ago. Paper is made by pulping (crushing up) rags or wood. The secret of papermaking took hundreds of years to spread around the world.

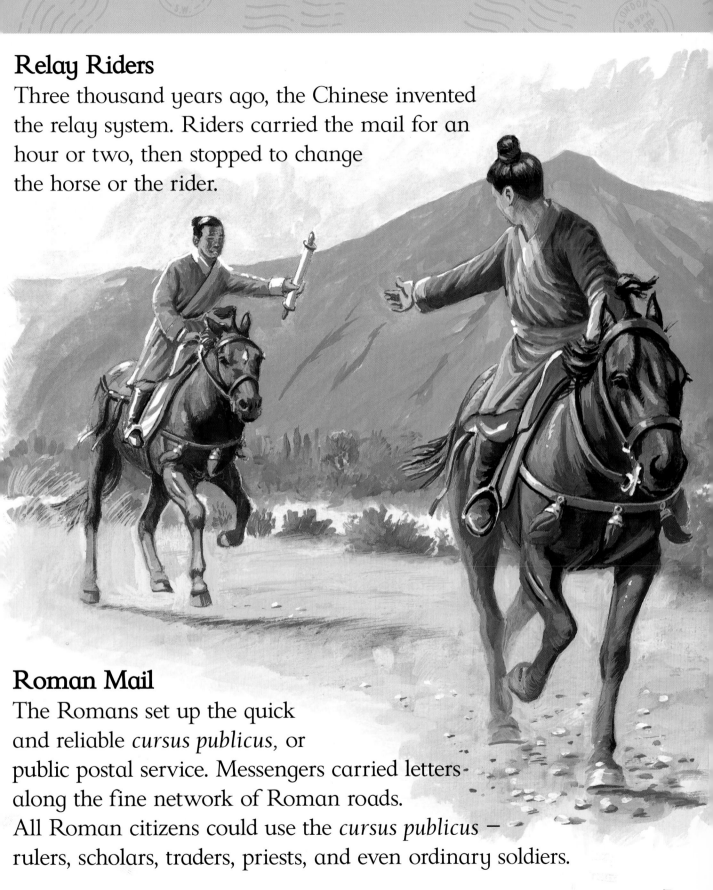

Relay Riders

Three thousand years ago, the Chinese invented the relay system. Riders carried the mail for an hour or two, then stopped to change the horse or the rider.

Roman Mail

The Romans set up the quick and reliable *cursus publicus,* or public postal service. Messengers carried letters along the fine network of Roman roads. All Roman citizens could use the *cursus publicus* — rulers, scholars, traders, priests, and even ordinary soldiers.

Signed and Sealed

The first letters were written with brushes. Early pens were made from reeds or large feathers, known as quills.

People used to make their own ink. It was made from all sorts of things, including soot and a dark juice taken from oak trees. Ink was stored in jars or in animal horns.

Writing with a quill and ink in the early seventeenth century.

Making a Quill Pen

Make sure an adult helps you with this project! You will need a goose feather, a sharp knife, paper, and ink.

1. Cut off the tip of the quill. Check that the inside is clean and hollow.

2. Make a vertical slit in the nib (end) of your quill.

3. Dip your pen in the ink, and get writing!

Seals

Since many people did not write their own letters, they needed a way to show that their letters were real. To do this, they put their own 'seal' (an image in wax) on their letters.

Making a Seal

The letter was written, then folded over two or three times. Hot, soft wax was dropped onto the letter to seal it. Then an image was pressed into the wax. When the wax cooled, it turned hard. The image was now fixed into the wax.

Wax seals kept a letter secret. This was very useful before envelopes were invented in the eighteenth century. If you received a letter with a broken seal, you knew someone had opened it before you!

During the Middle Ages, rulers, priests, the army, and the universities set up and ran their own postal services across Europe. There was a public service in northern Germany. Mounted mailmen blew on their horns as they rode through the villages. Anyone with letters to send would bring them out.

▶ A mailman delivering letters on foot in the Middle Ages.

▼ This seventeenth century German mailman blows a horn to announce his arrival.

Postboys

In Britain, innkeepers had to stable horses for use by the king's messengers. These messengers were called postboys. This service was only for the use of the king and government officials, but people across the country also kept horses for hire by messengers carrying letters for rich merchants and nobles.

These fifteenth century merchants have brought letters from abroad.

Expensive Postal Services

Early postal services were very expensive. The cost of delivering a letter depended on how far it was going and how heavy it was. The fee was paid by the person receiving the letter, not the one sending it. Only rich people sent and received letters.

Reliable Mail

The first truly national service was set up in 1464 by King Louis XI of France. During the sixteenth and seventeenth centuries, postal services across western Europe became much more reliable.

NEWS! NEWS!!

AARON OLIVER, Poſt-Rider, WISHES to inform the Public, that he has extended his Route; and that he now rides thro' the towns of Troy, Pittſtown, Hooſick, Mapletown, part of Bennington and Shaftſbury, Petersburgh, Stephentown, Greenbuſh and Schodack. All commands in his line will be received with thanks, and executed with punctuality. He returns his ſincere thanks to his former cuſtomers; and intends, by unabated diligence, to merit a continuance of their favours.

O'er ruggid bills, and vallies wide,
He never yet bas fail'd to trudge it:
As ſteady as the flowing tide,
He bands about the NORTHERN BUDGET.
June 18, 1799.

The New World

At the same time, people were beginning to look to the New World for a fresh start in life. In early colonial America, people depended on friends, merchants, and Native Americans to carry mail for them around the colonies. The first regular mounted mail service in America began in January 1673 between New York and Boston.

An early American mail-rider tells people about his service (1799).

Receiving Stations

People wanting to send a letter deposited it at special shops, coffeehouses, or inns that acted as receiving stations. Mail was then carried to other receiving stations for collection. It was not delivered to people's homes unless they paid an extra fee to a letter carrier.

A London postman with his bell (1820).

▲ A coffeehouse was the best place to send and receive mail in the 1700s.

Bellmen

In some cities, strolling bellmen walked through the streets. When people heard the bell ringing, they would bring out their letters. This saved them a visit to the receiving house.

Early mail was carried on foot or by mounted mailboys. But carrying mail alone could be dangerous. By the eighteenth century, many postal services carried the mail in horse-drawn coaches. The coaches carried passengers as well as mail. They traveled along special post roads that were better than the normal roads.

The Stage

Mail coaches made their journeys in stages, so they were also known as stagecoaches. At the end of each stage, they stopped at a coaching inn or a relay station. Here they changed horses and picked up or let off passengers and mail. Long-distance mail therefore took a long time to get to its destination.

The Pony Express

To speed up mail deliveries in the USA, the Pony Express mail service was set up in 1860. Mail was carried in saddle bags by brave young riders across the wild west of America. There were 80 riders, 430 horses, and 190 postal stations. The riders had to change horses in only two minutes. The journey time for the 2,000-mile (3,200-km) route was 11 days.

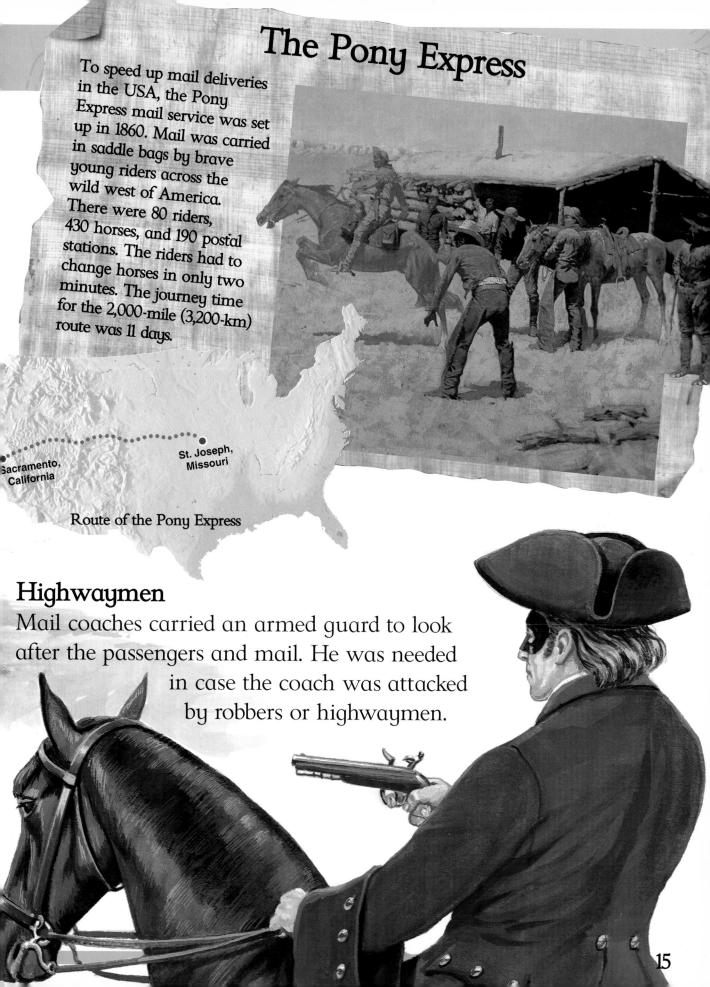

Sacramento, California

St. Joseph, Missouri

Route of the Pony Express

Highwaymen

Mail coaches carried an armed guard to look after the passengers and mail. He was needed in case the coach was attacked by robbers or highwaymen.

Post Offices

By the beginning of the nineteenth century, proper post offices were replacing the inns, shops, and coffeehouses as receivers and collectors of mail. But there were still few mailboxes.

London's busy general post office in 1849.

If you wanted to mail a letter, you had to take it to the nearest post office. There it would be weighed, and you would be charged depending upon how heavy it was and how far it was traveling. It became more common for the sender to pay the postage. Letters were stamped to show that postage had been paid.

Special Delivery

Letters would be delivered to the post offices of big cities, and people could either collect them for themselves or pay a little extra for the mail to be delivered to their door by carriers.

Country Mail

People living in country areas still had to collect their mail from the town post offices. This was difficult for these people, especially for those that lived in remote areas, where it could take many days to reach the nearest post office.

Sending letters was still very expensive, and most ordinary people could not afford to do it.

A nineteenth century American mailman runs to catch the mail as the stagecoach thunders past.

Stamps

In 1837 a man called Rowland Hill introduced a new way of sending the mail around Britain. He suggested that the post office should have a standard list of charges based on weight only, not distance, and that postage should only be paid by the sender. He also suggested that a label should be stuck on letters to show that prepayment had been made. The modern postage stamp was born!

Sir Rowland Hill.

Penny Post

In 1840 the British post office began charging one penny to deliver a normal letter anywhere in the country. The person sending the letter paid for, and stuck a one-penny stamp onto an envelope. People no longer had to pay letter carriers to deliver mail to their doors, wherever they lived. The idea was a great success.

Designing a Stamp

You will need paper, colored pencils or paints, scissors, and paste.

1. Draw the shape of your stamp on a piece of paper and color it in.

2. Write the value on your stamp and the country it has come from.

3. Cut out your stamp and stick it onto an envelope. But don't try to send a letter with your stamp on it!

Mailboxes

Other countries began using stamps. At last, everyone could afford to use the mail, and there was a huge increase in the number of letters. More and more mailboxes sprang up in towns and country areas.

Express Delivery

From the middle of the nineteenth century onward, several inventions greatly sped up the delivery of the mail. The first was the railway. Mail trains carried sacks of letters hundreds of miles in only a few hours. Mail wagons picked up mail without even stopping! Later, motor vans made delivery even quicker.

More than a hundred years separate the mail train advertised above, and this 1930s van.

Sorting Offices

As more people learned to read and write, they sent more letters. By 1900, millions of letters were delivered each day. More post offices were needed. More mailboxes were set up in towns and villages. Huge sorting offices were built to sort out the mail and send it to all the right addresses. Machines were invented to print postmarks and sort mail automatically.

▲ An American mailbox from the early 1900s.

◀ A British mailbox from the 1800s.

Mailboxes

In the past, when very few letters were sent, a letter was addressed with just a name and a town or district. Now that everyone was receiving letters, each house needed a name or number and a mailbox.

▼ Can you tell which of these letters is old and which is new?

Doctor B. Harrington
Beverley
East Riding of Yorkshire

Carla Rainer
Flat 5
17 Shatton Road
Eddington
Greater Manchester
M26 6AD

Overseas Mail

The first official international sea mail services started in the seventeenth century, linking the ports of Europe with their colonies overseas. Mail was also carried privately by ships' captains. The mail was collected in inns and coffeehouses in the ports where ships arrived and departed.

The mail for India is loaded onto this ship in the French port of Boulogne, in 1844.

In 1639 Richard Fairbanks' tavern in Boston became the official place for collection and receipt of mail arriving in Massachusetts from England. Other American states soon followed and set up official receiving stations for international mail.

Mail Steamers

Sea mail was carried in sailing ships. The service was not very reliable because it depended on the wind. The first steam ships were built in the nineteenth century. Mail steamers were quicker and more reliable than sailing ships.

Special Par
Delivery exprès

AIR MAIL
PAR AVION

By air mail
Par avion

By air mail
Par avion

Airmail

When airplanes were invented in the twentieth century, long-distance mail services became even faster. Airmail was first tried in 1911, and by the 1920s it was firmly established. By the 1990s a letter could be sent from America to Europe in just 24 hours.

Lawrence and Elmer Sperry Aviation Pioneers

US Airmail 39

Down the Wire

I n the nineteenth century, scientists invented a completely new way of sending messages. This was the telegraph. The words of a message were turned into electric signals and sent down a wire. At the other end of the wire, the signals were changed back into words.

An early machine for sending and receiving telegrams.

Morse Code

In 1843, Samuel Morse invented his famous Morse code for changing words into electric signals.

A B C D E F G H I J K L M

The code used short signals (dots) and long signals (dashes). An "A," for example, was a dot followed by a dash. A telegraph operator needed lots of practice to quickly turn a stream of dots and dashes into words. Later, a teleprinter did the job automatically.

N O P Q R S T U V W X Y Z

Telegraph Offices

Telegraph messages were sent to post offices or telegraph offices. The office receiving the message typed it out as a short letter, or telegram. This was delivered as quickly as possible. Since telegrams were expensive, they were used mainly for short and important messages, such as wedding congratulations or birth announcements.

International TELEGRAM

Peter Bendick
45 Dean Street
Farmdown
Doncaster
D12 3DG

MANCHESTER
6.V.97
M3

A telegraph office.

Today's Mail

The zip code is a modern invention. When we address an envelope, we finish with this code. Then our letter is ready for mailing (1).

After mail has been collected from a mailbox (2), it is taken to a sorting office.

Letters used to be sorted by hand. Nowadays, a machine puts electronic marks on the letters, according to their zip codes, to say where they are going (3).

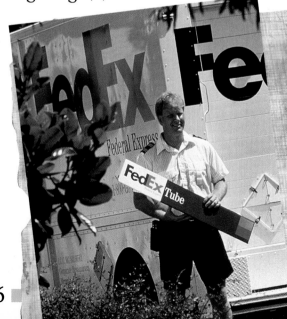

Courier Services

Couriers deliver thousands of letters, packets, and packages every day. In order to deliver their mail as quickly as possible, couriers take it by motorbike, van and airplane. They can carry a letter or package half way around the world and deliver it the very next morning.

Electronic Sorting

The letters move along a belt into a sorting machine that reads the marks. The machine steers all letters with similar marks into the same bag (4).

The bags are then taken by van, train, or aircraft (5), and carried to a sorting office where they will be delivered nearby.

Delivering Today's Mail

Here the letters are sorted again into districts, streets, and houses. Mailmen and mailwomen collect the letters for their own rounds and set off to deliver them. The journey finally ends when a letter comes through your mailbox, and you rush to see if it is for you (6).

On Screen

In the 1980s it became quite common to send letters by fax. Once a letter was written, it was fed into a fax machine. This scanned the letter and sent it to its address electronically. A fax machine at the other end printed it out, with no need for postal workers, sorting offices, or even stamps.

2 Message sent to local server.

②

How an e-mail message is sent.

1 Message typed in by person on computer.

E-Mail

By the 1990s there was yet another way of sending a letter. This was by e-mail. The letter was written straight onto a computer screen. It was then sent via the Internet directly to another computer and read on-screen. An e-mail letter traveled to the other side of the world in seconds. And no one had even used a pen and paper!

③

3 Message beamed up to orbiting satellite.

4 Message sent down to server close to destination.

④

⑥

⑤

6 Messages can even be relayed to a ship's computer.

5 Message relayed to computer and appears on screen.

Tomorrow's Mail

Today more letters are sent than ever before. But what will happen in the future? Perhaps a time will come when every home is on the Internet. Then, maybe, letters, envelopes, and stamps will be found only in museums.

Time Line

B.C.

c. 3500   Writing invented in Sumeria.
c. 2000   Postal system begins in Egypt.
c. 1000   Postal system begins in China.
c. 300   Egyptians using reed pens.

A.D.

c. 105   Tsai Lun makes the first paper.
c. 1500   Pencils being used.
1500s   Postal service running between
           Brussels, Vienna, and Madrid.
1721   Regular postal service between
           London and America begins.
1828   John Mitchell introduces machine-
           made steel pens.
1838   Mail first sorted on board a moving
           mail train.
1839   Electric telegraph invented.
1840   Penny post system begins.
1843   Morse code invented.
1860   Pony Express mail service set up
           in western USA.
1867   Christopher Scholes makes first
           reliable typewriter.
1884   L.E. Waterman makes the first reliable
           fountain pen.
1911   Air mail first tried.
1919   First air mail service begins
           between London and Paris.
1938   Ladislao Biro produces the first
           reliable ballpoint pen.
1946   First electronic computer built.
1960s   Pens with fiber tips introduced.
1969   First Internet set up.
1980s   Fax machines available for home use.
1990s   E-mail available for home use.

Glossary

Courier A special delivery service that takes mail all around the world as quickly as possible.

Papyrus A kind of paper made from reeds.

Parchment Dried animal skin used as paper.

Quill A long feather used as a pen.

Relay Delivering mail by passing it from one carrier to another.

Scribe Someone who does other people's writing for them.

Seal The wax image that a sender puts on a letter to prove that they have written it.

Sorting office An office where letters are sorted for delivery.

Stagecoach A coach that is pulled by different teams of horses during its journey.

Telegram A written message that is sent by telegraph.

Telegraph A way of sending a message down a wire by electricity.

Teleprinter A machine that prints out a message sent by telegraph.

Further Reading

Brimner, Larry Dane, *E Mail*, True Books, 1998

Burns, Peggy, *The Post*, Wayland, 1994

Farrell, Sue, *To the Post Office With Mama*, New York, 1994

Fyson, Nance, *History of Britain's Post*, Young Library, 1992

Landstrom, Olof, *Will Goes to the Post Office*, R & S Books, 1994

Thomson, Ruth, *In the Post*, Black, 1990

Ramsay, Helena, *Where Does a Letter Go?* Evans, 1996

Index